GET FAMOUS

The Greatest Resource for Mom Bloggers On the Planet

Make Money Fast with Your Blog
Have Advertisers Chase You Like Paparazzi
Get a Massive Following

Informative Tutorials
Amazing Resources
Simple to Read
Easy to Use
Massive Results

Lisa Cash Hanson
Mompreneur Mogul

Table of Contents

Introduction

First, I want to say thank you for buying my book. Writing it was one of the hardest things I've ever done. I want you to know that by buying this book you are not just buying tips or resources, you are helping my family and contributing to our dreams. I have many projects in my head and they all cost money. Money is always a blessing, but the most important receiver of that blessing is my beautiful daughter, Matilda. So in giving to us through purchasing this book, you have given to her, and from deep in my heart allow me to say, "Thank you!"

I'd also like to thank my husband, Chad. He has been an amazing support through this process. I have spent so much time away from him, staying awake all hours of the night trying to get this book completed.

I'd also like to give credit to Jesus, because without HIM I could do absolutely nothing. Every bit of success I have comes from

HIS grace and gifts on my life. If you don't know HIM, ask me and I'll introduce you to HIM.

And now to you: I thank you, my family thanks you, and I believe if you follow the suggestions in this book, you will have *The most amazing blog on the planet*!

GET FAMOUS has been both a joy and an incredible challenge to write. Many of you have emailed and asked questions over the past months regarding your blogs. I try to get to every one but it's just impossible. I have many projects I'm working on and as most of you know, a baby is more than a full time job. I've invested countless hours pouring over my own articles and other resources in order to create the most helpful content I can provide and answer many of those questions. I trust this book will live up to its name: *Get Famous - The Most Amazing Blogger's Resource On The Planet.*

Even though I have spent many hours typing past 2 a.m. to put this book together, it was worth it. You are worth it. When you are done reading this book, I could really use your help. Please, **take the time to write a review on** my page (see link). It would mean so much to me. GET FAMOUS REVIEW

GET FAMOUS
SUBSCRIBE NOW
Breathe BLOG
Be Amazing

When I decided to create this book, my purpose was to fill it with powerful and practical tips you can use. Applying these tips will increase your blog's success. I've had countless moms ask questions ranging from, "How did you make money so fast with your blog?" to "I really need some tips on how to get more followers." No matter what your question is, I know you will love this eBook and, believe me, by the time we're finished, this will help you and your blog GET FAMOUS.

Please visit me on Facebook at Mompreneur Mogul and Twitter @Mompreneurmogul and tell me your thoughts on the book. If you have questions, please visit my blog at the bottom of this page and send a note.

Dedication

This book is dedicated to my amazing husband, Chad. Without his support this book would not have been possible. To our beautiful baby girl, Matilda, who is just 10 months old, but one day may read this. My mother who has always encouraged me to dream big and has always been my greatest fan even when I've failed.

I love you all.

This book is also dedicated to you. Those who follow my blog, comment, read my newsletters, and are a constant source of encouragement and support. I truly appreciate you. I am thankful for each and every one of you.-Lisa

Blogging Basics

What About Blogging?

What is a blog? According to Wikipedia, it's a personal journal published on the World Wide Web. According to me, it's like an online diary, newspaper, or notepad - you get the picture, right?

You update it regularly. Some update every day, every three days, or once a week.

There is a sense of community because people come and comment on your blog.

Your Blog Content

Well, here we go. What are you going to write in those big empty spaces on your Blogger or Wordpress site? It's totally up to you. It's your world and everyone else is just living in it.

You will hear the word *niche* everywhere in the blogosphere. I didn't pick mine. Believe it or not, it picked me.

I wrote about my life and some tips, but I added a poll asking readers what they wanted: blogging tips, parenting, or humor. Oddly enough, the result was about 75% blog tips, 15% parenting, and 10% humor. I think people should laugh more, but this is what they chose.

If you want to know what a *niche* is, it's a specific topic that your posts will revolve around.

Ask yourself: Who will read my blog and what topic can I write about forever? It may not be forever, but it's important to find a subject you are truly passionate about. That passion will drive you towards your niche.

Quick Tip: In order to give a more polished and professional appearance, get your own domain name. A dot com is always better than a dot blogspot.

Your Blog's Sidebar

Most blogs have a sidebar, and some have two. You can put anything you you want on your sidebar, but here are a few suggestions:

- A way to subscribe to the blog's RSS feed
- A way to subscribe to the blog's mailing list
- A search bar
- A list of the recent posts
- A list of the most popular posts
- The categories
- A list of the most recent comments
- Social profile buttons
- Ads

Your Blogging Goals

You will want to set a few goals. I think goals are a powerful tool. They should be flexible, however, because as soon as you start blogging you'll probably generate new ideas. Be open to change.

For example, here are some of my goals:

• Write an eBook
• Get 1000 followers in 6 months
• Teach a class online
• Start a Blog Tribe (look for the tribe section in this book.)
• Start an online Mom Vlog show

These are a few examples; yours can be anything your little heart desires. As I said, it's your world and everyone else is just visiting. BUT be sure you make everything appealing to your readers, because after all, who wants to live in a world all by themselves?

Blogging Nuggets

Be patient. It may take a little time to get traffic, make money, and have a following. It can also happen overnight. I made money and landed a major interview in under two months. I'm not bragging, I'm telling you it's possible.

Be consistent. Keep up with your schedule. If you blog on the first of the month and don't do another post until two months later, chances are you'll have a hard time attracting traffic. People like active blogs.

Be yourself. It's cool you are reading my book, but I'm me and you're you. Don't try to be anyone else, because then the world of blogging will be robbed of your super cool style.

Don't get discouraged. Don't get discouraged. Don't get discouraged. That was not a typo. I really want you to get that. If your blog isn't taking off the way you'd like, just focus on maybe two tips a week and do those, then next week two more. Don't allow yourself to get discouraged. It's just wasted energy. And don't become overwhelmed because before you know it you'll have a spectaculicious blog.

Blogging Communities

http://www.momdot.com/

http://www.topmommyblogs.com/

http://www.blogher.com/

http://www.thesitsgirls.com/

http://www.blogaholicnetwork.com/

http://www.mombloggersclub.com/

http://www.momblogsociety.com/

What are Blogging Communities, why do you need them, and what do you do with them?

The lists of these sites are endless, really. Blogging communities are usually started by mom bloggers. They form them as a way to get bloggers together to socialize, promote their blogs, increase traffic, and teach new skills for blogging.

Many of them have classes available where you can learn some cool techniques. There are a ton of options on some of these communities. I belong to each of these and you should too.

Each one offers something unique. They've all been great to me in their unique ways - SITS girls has featured me and sent paid posts my way. I can't thank Tiffany enough. Trisha from Momdot has a killer forum that you will love. I've taught her 30 day blog challenge; it was amazing and so is she.

Emily from Blogaholic Social Network has featured me numerous times, love her. So has Tiffany from Bloggy Moms, and each of them drive traffic to my site. Ladonna from Mom Blog Society is super personable & willing to help. She's fab!

Of course, you realize there are numerous Blogging Communities. These are just a few of my favorites. Just Google "mom blogging communities" and many will pop up.

Tips For Using Communities

• Add your blog posts on their sites to help gain new readers for your own blog.

• Join groups. Most sites have a list of groups they offer:

Groups for giveaways, bloggers with less than a hundred followers, bloggers who follow on Twitter, working moms, Christian moms, stay-at-home moms, moms who work out, moms who dance in tutus (okay, not really that last one, I'm just making sure you are paying attention). Nearly any group you can think of, you will find there.

• You can promote yourself as an expert by welcoming new members and letting them know they can come to you with questions. You'll feel great for helping someone else and they'll be happy to follow someone who is really generous with their expertise.

• Share your giveaways to draw more followers to your blog.

Blog communities are also great for guest blogging. As with BSN or SITS Girls I have been featured using these blogging communities.

As a member of a blogging community you may have the opportunity to:

• Receive numerous offers for guest posts.
• Get recruited to be a paid blogger.
• Gain some awesome new friends.
• Start your own Tribe.

What's a Tribe? Glad you asked. Please see the next chapter.

Blog Tribes

Think of your blogging tribe as something from the movie *Ya Ya Sisterhood*. It's a group of bloggers who get together for the common goal of promoting one another's blogs. It's like the old saying that two heads are better than one. Well, eight bloggers sharing tweets about each other's blog are better than you going it alone.

Every tribe has its owns rules (or no rules depending on who is the leader of that tribe.) On certain days they work to promote posts, giveaways, or other important issues within that tribe to social media, multiplied by the eight bloggers. (or whatever the number of people in a tribe.) It's good to keep the tribe a little smaller. That way, you are sure to get the attention you need. However, some tribes are as large as twelve members or more.

7 Steps to Building A Solid Tribe

1. Make your bloggy friends feel welcome. Everyone likes to feel important, so show them they are. Reply to comments as snappily as you can. It's great blogging etiquette and it will make them feel warm and fuzzy.

2. Reward subscribers with a cool freebie like a report or copy of your eBook. And make it personal. A special gift for your subscribers only. Surprise people. I love surprises. You

can do this by sending a special note from time to time, re-tweeting something that really matters to them, bragging about their blog in one of your posts and more. Get creative.

3. Reward tribe members for the awesome work they do on your blog. Like I said, we all love to be loved so start showing some affection and tell those bloggers how much they truly mean to you. For those of you who follow me, let me just say to MY followers, you are one in a million and I am so truly thankful for each and every one of you!

4. Use Featured Follower once a week, or month and highlight one of your more dedicated followers with a review of their work and, of course, a link. The new LinkyFollower tool in my resource page has a cool feature for that. Check it out.

5. Go with the friends you have today. Sometimes the greatest tribe members you can have are the ones who faithfully comment on your blog now. You know who they are; they are supportive, they work hard to share great things with others about you and your blog. Those are the friends who make the best tribe members.

You can find Tribes on Facebook - I have one called The Soaring Bloggeristas.

You can also find tribes at http://www.triberr.com

Blog Hop Tutorial

What is a blog hop? A blog hop is a way to meet new bloggers and increase your blog's traffic.

It's a great way to find new mom blogs, learn blogging tips, and promote your blog. This is a brief tutorial on what a blog hop is and how to join one.

How do you join? You will see many different blogs listed. They call it a hop because you "hop" from on blog link to the next. This one is called, "Tis the Season Blog Hop."

You click on the link to the blog hop, usually the main page of the person who is hosting the hop. Here is an example of what it looks like: This is from a Linky Tool Blog Hop not all hops look the same please keep that in mind during this tutorial.

Link up a post that is based around this time of year:
Christmas, Hanuka, winter activities, decoration ideas, posts about traditions, Holiday recipes, Winter photos, **Winter bucket list**, Holiday cards and crafts, etc......anything **Winter** or Holiday **themed!**

Once you add your blog- stop by a few other blogs on the list to follow and leave a comment, let them know you are stopping by from BSN so they know you are a new friend and can connect with you on the community as well!

Feel free to Tweet about the linkup, post it on Facebook, **or even grab the code for your blog (the code is located below the linky list) a great way to fill up a post for a day ;) If you add it to your blog please copy the full post so others know the rules.**

If you don't want to grab the full post and linky code feel free to grab a blog hop badge!

```
<a
href="http://www.blo
gaholicnetwork.com
```

The blog hop will be open until 12/27/11

Happy Holidays!

This is a **Blog Hop!**

Once you are on the page, you will see a section that says, "Add your link." It looks like this:

Add your link
(Submissions close in 1d 2h 31m)

URL: _____ (URL of your blog post)

Name: _____

Email: _____ (Not visible)

Submit link

Trouble linking up?
Try here

continue to the next page...............

You will then see an image like this:

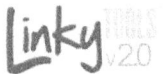 **Thumbnail Linky**

You'll choose a thumbnail image in the next step, but first...
enter the following information to get started.

1.   Link it to: http://

Example:
http://www.riggsfamilyblog.com/2009/01/about-abby.html

2.   Enter a caption or title that will show up below your thumbnail:

Caption
or Title:

(maximum 45 characters)

3.   Optional: Include your email address.

Your email:

A note about your email privacy

Optional: Include your name.

Your name:

4.

⊙ Let me crop my own image   ○ Auto crop my image

Explanation

Get an image
from the web page link   **From Web**
you entered above in #1:

Use an image from a file   **From File**
on your computer:

Add your blog's URL in the space provided. For example, my URL is http://www.mompreneurmogul.com/. You can also use the URL to one of your blog posts. You do this by clicking on your blog post then copying and pasting the code in your search bar above.

In the name portion, type the name of your blog. For example, I would, type: Mompreneur Mogul. Then type your email and click "submit."

Next, you should see your link appear. It should look like my example below.

49. Girliemom

50. Christmas Survey Part 1

51. How to Engage Toddlers in Christmas

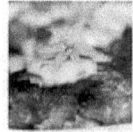
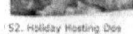
52. Holiday Hosting Dos and Donts

53. Your Family Should Have a Show - Santa Claws

54. The Jolly Blogger

55. Christmas Tree Pictures Blog Hop

56. Gingerbread Biscotti Recipe YUM!

57. MompreneurMogul Matildas first Christmas Tree

And that's it! Now you've joined your first blog hop and you can click on any of the other mom bloggers' links to check out new friends and gain new followers.

Visit my website to see if there is one happening now.
http://www.mompreneurmogul.com/

 If for any reason you do not see one available, just contact me via my blog and I'll point you in the right direction.

I

How To Make A Blog Button

Making a blog button is fairly simple. There are several steps but don't worry. Let's go through them.

There are lots of blogs that have a button like this with a scrolling text box underneath that houses the button's code. This makes it easy for other people to place your blog's button on their blog and link effortlessly to you.

This was mine.

A Blog Button is a cool picture you can use to promote your blog. You can share links for blog hops, giveaway links, or use them for putting on another blogger's blog. By doing this, you are creating a link between the two blogs.

Normally, if a person puts your button up, you'll put one up for them as well. A picture with a link is really the best description of a blog button.

Under the blog button you will often see a small box with some html code inside. This is the grab box, the part a person needs to copy in order to place the other person's blog button into their own blog (not too confusing, I hope). Most bloggers create buttons for blog hops, giveaway links, and link parties. This is a routine habit for promoting their blogs, making new blogging friends and finding new readers for their blog, as well as finding new blogs to read.

Fortunately, for you and for me, this is where my tutorial for a blog button ends. Don't worry. I've asked another one of my wonderful blogging friends, Amy Lynn Andrews, to help you out, so you can visit her link below to learn more.

Blogging With Amy How To Make A Blog Button Tutorial

Comment Your Way To Success

Here are some useful tips to help you get a great conversation going and increased traffic by way of comments:

• Be the first to comment. Digg is a great place to comment, especially if you can find a story that's listed on the front page. People rarely read the 20th comment so try to be the first and you should see an increase in traffic.
• Technorati has a list of the top 100 blogs on the internet. Find the blogs related to your topic and leave great comments. Don't spam or add links everywhere, people don't like that.
• When commenting, try to find the larger blogs that are similar to yours.

• Comment on at least 5 blogs every night

• Make sure you are adding to the discussion and not just saying, "Hey, I came to your blog, so come to mine." To me that's like someone saying, "I'll show you mine if you show me yours." Umm... No thanks. Gross! Check out these two articles for tips:

Powerful Tips To Building a Loyal Blog Following
http://www.mompreneurmogul.com/2011/12/5-powerful-tips-to-building-a-loyal-blog-following.html

How To Get Noticed In A Sea Of Self Promoters
 http://www.mompreneurmogul.com/2012/01/number-one-blogging-tip-how-to-get-noticed-in-a-sea-of-self-promoters.html

• Ask for comments. Simple isn't it?

• Ask questions in the body of your post. Things like, "What do you think? What would you have done?" and so on.

• Comment on other blogs daily. I know I already said that, it's an important point to remember.

• Use Comment Luv & Reply Me these are plugins on Wordpress. (for Wordpress users)

• **CommentLuv** allows you to 'share the love' with those who comment by showing their blog feed under the comment. I can't say how many times I've clicked on someone's CommentLuv feed simply because it showed a great blog title.

  • **ReplyMe** sends your individual reply to a commenter. With this plugin, the individual is guaranteed to know you appreciate them stopping by and allows you to further the discussion, especially if you integrate questions to that person in your reply.

- Reply to the comments left on your site.

- Write Catchy Titles.

- Publish unfinished content. You don't have to do this all the time, but if you say everything, there is nothing for anyone else to add.

- Make it easy for people to comment. I can't stand Captchas. I think they get in the way, but that's just me.

- **The most important thing to remember**: Behind every comment is a person. Behind every person is a life. Behind every life we all crave the same things. Attention, acceptance, love, laughter, hope, healing, kindness, strength, and respect. If you keep these things in mind when responding to your followers, you will reap great rewards and rich friends. Not in the financial sense, but in friends who will walk through the fire just for you.

Can You please do A favor for me? I would love your thoughts about this book and how it has helped you. If you'd like to write a short review, please send it to my email because I'd love to use your testimony in my next book or on my website.
lisa@mompreneurmogul.com

Creating Great Content

You will hear this over and over as it is the blogger's sacred mantra. Content, content, content. Creating great content is really the yin to the yang, the French fries to the burger, the toy to the Happy Meal. Have I made my point? Content really does matter. Your blog will be no different. Having great content will keep readers coming back.

 I also need to add that the frequency in which you decide to post is a factor to your blogs success. You have to keep your blog updated or your readers will get bored. Bored readers leave. I blog daily, sometimes twice or more per day. You'll find your own rhythm but make sure that you blog consistently.

I'm aware that you may find it challenging to pump out that amazing content. Here are some tips and tricks to help you along the way.

• Republish old content. Take an older existing article, and make it more current. Do this by adding and updating the article. Then publish it as a new, fresh article. This method won't work if you've only been blogging for a few months, but in time you will be able to do this occasionally.

- Ask your readers to write. Today I decided I wanted my readers to write tips about <u>Pinterest.</u> It's a great way to get unique content and every blogger loves a new audience.

- Use Guest Posts. It is so easy to find blogger who would like to write a guest post. Another great resource I use frequently is <u>Linkedin</u>. I belong to a few groups and one is actually called *"Guest Blogger"*. It's a great resource.

Patterns Of Crazy Popular Bloggers

Crazy popular bloggers are passionate about their niche. Here is a way to test your passion. Blog frequently whether you ever make any money from your site or not. This is how you know you truly love to blog. If you sit home and cry while eating chocolate because you haven't struck it rich, blogging might not be your passion.

Engage your readers. They took the time to write to you, so make sure you respond. Be encouraging and uplifting to them when you respond. Check your emails. Ask for their feedback; they will appreciate it. By doing this you may find some great tips along the way.

Try not to focus on link building all the time. Some bloggers are so worried about their Google Page Rank it makes their brain sizzle. I've already shared with you many opportunities I've received with a ZERO Google Page Rank. Readers matter more than rank. In case you are wondering, it was a Zero because my blog was less than three months old.

Be original. I cannot state this enough. I really get bored when I see the same title posts rehashed all over the blog world. If you want your blog to be successful then create your own brand. What is that brand? You. There is no other human on the face of the planet who is like you. Use that to your advantage.

Tell your story. Make your blog your very own special place and have every story told through the reflection of your eyes. That will make your blog a powerhouse.

Be the best writer you can be. I strive to improve in this area all the time. It's not professional to be sloppy so make sure that your blog is not sloppy either.

Don't attack others. Ignore nasty comments. I just had a situation with a super mean commenter. I chose not to allow the comment on my blog. I have read from other guru bloggers that they do post negative comments. Why? Because they know their readers will jump to their defense. It causes controversy. Controversy brings traffic and traffic equals more readers.

The choice is up to you to allow negative comments or not. Either way, don't attack the mean person in retaliation. My friend has a great saying:
"Don't wrestle in the mud with a pig. You'll get dirty and the pig will like it."

Update: During the writing of my book I had more negative comments to deal with than I ever thought possible. Read here to check out the story: The Best And The Worst Day Of My Blogging Life.

Hosting Giveaways

An effective blog giveaway should benefit all parties involved- the reader, the sponsor, and the blogger. The reader gets something free, the sponsor gets increased traffic or product interest, and you get more hits. In theory, that's how it's all supposed to work. If you've had a few giveaways under your belt, you know that there can be a few glitches along the way. I'm not an expert in this area and I can only share what worked for me. Here are a few tips:

Find Awesome Items to Give Away

The better the item, the more attention your giveaway will garner.

- If I'm approached directly by PR or marketing representatives or business owners and receive an intriguing pitch that doesn't specifically mention a giveaway opportunity, I ask for one.

- Email the company directly, tell them you love their product, and ask if they're interested in doing a giveaway.

Traffic numbers help so that they can see the benefit, of course. I just had a company send a note saying, "We know you're not on page one of Google but we like the look of your blog. Can we put an ad with you?" You don't need stats to be successful. You just need to "look" successful and then you will be.

Streamline Giveaway Admin

- Keeping track of what you're giving away can be tricky, especially when you've got several giveaways lined up. Scheduling and tracking giveaways using Google Calendar or a similar tool will help keep it all straight. It will also help ensure that you don't schedule a giveaway that will end while you're on vacation or otherwise unavailable.

- Most giveaway entries occur within the first two days of a giveaway. That said, they don't have to drag on forever. Play around with shorter giveaways. Try a one-day or three-day period.

- Use Google Docs to create an entry form for your readers. This prevents readers' email addresses from being harvested by blog-crawling harvester bots.

- Use http://www.rafflecopter.com/ it's one of the most amazing and easiest tools you can use if you want to host a giveaway. Visit the website to learn more.

- I've used <u>Random.org's integer generator</u> to choose a random winner. It's quick and easy, and since you've collected entries on a spreadsheet, finding the winning entry is a breeze, too.

- When choosing your winner, give them a limited length of time to respond to your notification email. Forty eight hours is the normal response time for most contests.

Help The Sponsor Out

Boost your giveaway's value to the sponsor by creating a reason for readers to visit the sponsor's site. Ask them to choose their favorite product from the sponsor's site and then come back and enter it into your entry form. Send them on a mini scavenger hunt. Your sponsor will love the extra traffic and sales that result, opening the door for additional giveaway opportunities.

Advertise

Make sure you advertise your giveaway. There are forums on the blogging communities I named above specifically for that purpose.

Here are a couple sites you can use:

www.online-sweepstakes.com

www.prizey.net

www.tipjunkie.net

www.contestgirl.com

Remember to utilize your social media avenues as well. These are but a few sites to get you started. Turn to "Google" to find more.

Vlogging

What is Vlogging or a Vlog? Imagine instead of writing your post, you videotape your post and speak your text. That is vlogging. But it doesn't have to be rehearsed. It can be a simple message, an introduction to a product, or just a review of your day. Here is an example of mine.

http://www.mompreneurmogul.com/2011/12/v-blog-family-photo-shoot-funny-with-my-husbands-narration.html

If you have a flip video camera or you use a Mac, it takes two minutes to record, plug it in to the computer, save, upload to Youtube, get embedded code, and launch on your blog. If you don't have a Mac you can still record, save the video, upload to Youtube, and post it on your blog. You can also skip the Youtube step all together and just post the video on your blog.

It's that simple. But here are some tips to help make your Vlog much better.

- Watch your backgrounds. No one expects Steven Spielberg, but if you have clutter in your background it's distracting. Try to make it as professional as possible. You want them to hear you, not think, "Is that the toilet behind her?"

- Sound is important. Lots of background noise takes away from your message. Loud music playing, dogs barking, the TV running - none of this should happen. When you make a video, quiet on the set!

- Get cleaned up. Unless you are doing the guy from "Dirty Jobs," you need to look put together. Hair combed, makeup on, look great. If we turned on the news and they were speaking in their pajamas, we would never take them seriously. So don't do this to your readers. Look professional. And by professional I don't mean you have to be in a suit or business attire, just look presentable.

- Try not to ramble. Be focused, be concise and be clear. You have a message. Deliver that message in a strong and powerful way. Keep in mind that lots of um's, or pauses are also distracting.

If you just follow these simple tips you'll have a great Vlog.

I Made $250.00 Dollars Blogging In One Month

One of the biggest questions I receive from bloggers (besides how do I get media for my blog) is, "How can I make money with my blog?"

There many ways to monetize your blog. Only you can figure out which method works best for your niche.

Here are just a few:

1. Affiliate programs

Affiliate marketing is a marketing practice in which a business rewards one or more affiliates for each visitor or customer brought in by the affiliate's own marketing efforts.

I will be adding some of these affiliate links to go with my GET FAMOUS book, which you are reading right now, so be sure to click here to find details in the future: http://www.mompreneurmogul.com/?portfolio=314

There are also many people who offer affiliate programs.The easiest way to find new affiliate programs is simply via Google just type in your topic - affiliate program - and you'll have many options.

You can also visit:

www.clickbank.com
http://www.100best-affiliate-programs.com/
http://www.affiliateseeking.com/

2. AdSense

Google **AdSense is a "contextual" advertising program** where publishers simply add a piece of code to their blogs that helps Google analyze what your page is about, so they can serve ads on that topic. This increases the chances of your readers clicking the ad, which increases the chances you'll earn income from them.

3. **eBook Sales**

You are reading an example of an eBook right now. You create your own eBook, and then you upload and sell it on your website. If you'd like more info on this topic, just email me and let me know that you are interested. You can also do a Google search "How To Write Your Own eBook"

4. Membership Sites

This is where you add value for your subscribers and you generate a monthly income based upon their memberships. It would be a paid member only site.

There are some great plugins if you wish to do this and is yet another reason I'm so in love with Wordpress. Here is a link for more information if you are interested: http://winkpress.com/membership-plugin/

5. Sponsorships/ Paid Reviews

This is how I've made money with my blog. People or companies email you asking if you would review their product, and they will pay you a set fee.

A big question bloggers always seem to have is "How much should I charge?" It depends. How much traffic does your site get? Don't allow stats to get in the way, however, of making money. Let me tell you about a recent experience.

I was looking at some of my group posts on LinkedIn. A President of a new toy company was looking for bloggers to do a review. He wanted them to have a high Google page rank. That means when you search for their niche their blog is on the first or second page of Google.

My blog was very new and I didn't have that high rank. My girlfriend did. I wrote him to tell him about my friend. He was thankful, then said this "I will get in touch with her." Then he said, "I saw your site and love how professional it looks. Would you be interested in doing a review for us also?"
Of course I told him, "Yes". Even though I didn't have the high page rank, I was still able to receive a free toy in the mail to review. It was an awesome product by the way.

(**Addition:** During the writing of this book my Yahoo! Shine feature aired. I jumped from 1700 visitors to over 14,000 and in just a few days I now have a 2 Google Page Rank. You can read about the highs and lows here : *The Best And The Worst Day Of My Blogging Life*)

Always remember everything is a negotiation. There really are no hard rules with your blog. It's your blog and your business. You make the rules.
You can also view other websites and locate people willing to pay you to post reviews or talk about their product.

You can find some of those opportunities here:

http://socialspark.com/

http://www.reviewme.com/

6. Freelance writing

This is when you get paid to blog for other websites. This is also how I've made some of my money. It depends on the site, but it could be anywhere from $10 per post on up.

I started this chapter by saying how quickly I made over $225 in one month. Let me tell what I did.

I want you to keep in mind my blog was only one month old, I had a ZERO Google Rank and about two million Alexa Rank. I also did not have one single ad on my blog.

1. I created my blog. This may seem like a simple step, but if you don't have a blog, you can't make any money. So start creating.

2. I created posts and lots of them. No one wants to come to an empty blog. That's like opening the Sunday paper and the cover looks good but inside there are no articles - you'd throw the paper out. This could be happening to some of your blogs right now. If you don't have enough content, start posting. Make sure to add great content. You can also ask other bloggers to provide guest posts for you in order to build quality content quickly.

3. I joined a few of the blogging communities that I already mentioned.

4. I posted everywhere. I tweeted, I commented on other blogs, I posted in forums, I posted in groups, I posted on Facebook, I posted on LinkedIn.

Then suddenly I received emails like this:

"I found Mompreneur Mogul while researching popular mom & craft blogs and absolutely love your work! I am currently working on editorial outreach and feel that the audience of your blog would benefit from reading about them."

"I came across your blog and thought I would reach out to you. I am the Editorial Director of a new website geared towards moms, ParentSociety.com, and I was hoping that you might be interested in becoming a regular blogger for us." -Editor Parent Society

"Hi Lisa,

Our company Sneakpeeq, is the largest and fastest growing social shopping company on Facebook. I am reaching out to you in hopes of partnering with Mompreneur Mogul. We absolutely love your blog!"- Henry President Sneekpeeq

"Greetings

This e-mail is to contact you about
being on our radio show to do a phone
interview for our Talk Radio Show."

These are only a few examples of pitch letters I've been sent. I've also been featured in **Yahoo! Shine**, Sitsgirls, Blogaholic, Social Network, Mogulized, Women Entrepreneur, & more.

I did this all by myself. No agent, no PR rep, no other assistants just myself. This is why I am totally confident - if I did it so can you. It was easy.

When it comes to making money with your blog, you are only limited by your imagination.

You can do blog edits and charge money for that service (many do this for free, but if you build a reputation, you can charge for it.)

Email Consulting- (You charge fees to help people via email.)

Product reviews.

And the list just goes on and on.

The first thing you have to realize is that it is very possible. The second thing you need to realize is that it's very easy. If you think it's hard, then it will be. Just believe it's easy and soon you'll see results come pouring in. Don't give up!

Media Kits

What is a blog media kit?

Your media kit is a resume for your blog. It is a package of information that introduces your blog to interested advertisers and answers their questions about it.

What does it do?

A media kit acts as a sales tool for selling advertising on your blog. Your blog media kit should be used to get potential advertisers pumped up about advertising on your blog.

Create your kit as a professional-looking document that advertisers can download from your blog, that you can send out to companies that contact you, and that you can send out to companies you contact directly.

What should I include in the blog media kit?

The blog media kit should provide advertising rates, key demographics, blog traffic information, and your contact details. (If you are unfamiliar with these terms, don't worry. You can google anything and everything, so take a minute and do that if you are lost. Also, remember I didn't have a media kit and at the time of writing this I still don't. Yet I have made plenty of money.

Your media kit should include everything a potential advertiser might need to know to help them decide to buy advertising space on your blog.

Blog profile

Describe your blog, define your blog values, describe your blog content, and describe yourself.

Blog target audience/traffic

Getting visitors to your blog matters. Who wants to set up a store in a neighborhood where no one lives? Same thing with your blog. Your blog traffic and your blog target audience motivate advertisers.
You will share your blog traffic stats, number of RSS subscribers, and number of email newsletter subscribers.

SEO

When people search the Internet for specific keywords relevant to your potential advertiser and suddenly they end up on your blog, you have a key selling point. One of the most powerful strategies of selling advertisements is to show the potential sponsor how you rank in search engines for their product / service related keywords.

Advertising options / rates

Let the potential advertiser know what kind of advertising options you offer on your blog. Include the position of ads, the size of ads. Show it by including a screenshot which has the potential ad position marked. Do not forget to include pricing for each of these ads.

I could give you advice on how much you should charge for ads, however, I have found there are too many factors involved. I think you should make your own decisions regarding how much you charge for ad space. I will point out a few things that will help you with your decision:

- Size & location of ad space
- How many visitors your page receives
- Your page rank

Again those are just a few factors. Additional research will give you a much better idea.

Contact details

Finally, make sure that you include all the contact details needed in order for the company or individual to get in touch with you.

How To Get Media Exposure

By far the most popular question, aside from "How do I make money with my blog?" is, "How can I get press opportunities like you have?"

So here it is a nutshell. A super-sized nutshell, because I will be giving you a lot of information here. There are a number of sites that you can sign up for free and you will get bi-weekly emails, or sometimes daily of leads, from journalists. This is very cool because if you are what they are looking for, you will have a terrific opportunity.

The first one is http://www.reporterconnection.com/ Visit this link and sign up for emails. You will get leads that look like the ones below. These are very old, so don't waste your time. Just go to the above link, sign up, and get the brand new leads.

Timely Topics (in the ~~news~~)

1. Three Murders, Seven Dead In 36 Hours - Law Experts Needed *(KARN-FM Talk Radio)*
2. Pro/Con: Does Black History Promote Racism? *(Victoria Advocate)*
Business & Finance

3. Have Any Marketing Tips/Ideas For Private Practice Doctors? *(PracticeDock Doctor Marketing Blog)*
4. Problems With Salary History? Please Share *(WorkWise Interactive)*
Food & Cooking

5. Looking For Homemade Dog Food Recipes *(A Novice With Moxie)*
Health, Nutrition & Fitness

The next source is my favorite: HARO Help A Reporter Out.

http://www.helpareporter.com/

For everyone who has asked how I got the Yahoo Finance interview, where they flew from NY to Las Vegas to film me, this is it.

If you want to see behind-the-scenes takes from the day, you can click here. Yahoo Finance Film Shoot With Mompreneur Mogul

This is how it happened: I signed up for these services. A great lead came from HARO. I submitted a proposal via email, they liked it, forwarded to the producers. They did a Skype casting call with Chad and myself, then they showed the producers, who loved us, and we were on camera for an entire day. That is how it worked.

Quick Tips:

• Only submit what you really qualify for. If you're a mom blogger, do not submit for technical gadgets, even if it says National TV Show.

• Reporters are very busy, so don't waste their time. It also reflects poorly if you apply for a project you know you're not right for.

• When journalists send out queries on HARO Reporter Connection, often if you are one of the first pitches to arrive, you could be the one scoring the interview.

- Don't be afraid to pitch often. Sometimes it's a numbers game, and the more stories you submit yourself for the better your odds of getting exposure.
- Target the right editors. If you blog about food, don't pitch a fashion magazine. Enough said.

• Be sure to network. You never know who may know someone who is looking for a blogger like you, so be social - it will pay greatly.

You will love both of these services and you may get some wonderful opportunities from it.

Additional Media Tips

Enter your profile on
http://www.profnetconnect.com

It's a place where PR, journalists, and bloggers share information. This portion is free, so add your profile today.

One of the other ways to get in the press is to start a collection of posts on your blog that people find fascinating. Many bloggers have been picked up by publications just because they wrote an interesting series that was getting a lot of attention.

You can also go through http://muckrack.com/ and find regional or national reporters on Twitter who cover your niche.

Be prepared before the pitch

Sum up your story in one sentence.

Think of who will be reading or watching your story so you know to how you focus your pitch. Think of what they would want to hear.

Study to find breaking news that's relevant to your industry.

Don't forget your local reporters. Many times they need fresh stories too.

Write and submit press releases. I did not have a press release when Yahoo wanted to interview me, so it's possible to get press without one. But they never hurt.

I found the following article while doing some research, and although some bloggers are afraid to point their readers to another blog, I am not. I want to help you more than I want to keep you all to myself. I know my tips work, many have testified to that. I want to share something else with you. This is one of the best articles I've found on getting intel on media and how to pitch the press. When you read it you'll understand why.

http://www.shoemoney.com/2010/09/14/getting-press-for-your-website-application-or-service/

How To Write A Press Release

1. Create a Compelling Title

When you are at the grocery store look at magazines. What titles grab your attention? It is the same for a reporter. They get hundreds, if not thousands, of pitches. Make sure that yours is the one they pay attention to. If you want to learn more about writing and titles, I urge you to visit http://www.copyblogger.com/blog/

Reporters are very busy. Answer the following classic questions in your press release and it will increase your chance for success: **Who, what, when, where and why**. Then find the story hook that will help *them* write a story their readers won't forget.

2. Tips for Headlines

As I said, read Copyblogger for tips on writing a compelling headline.

You can only make one first impression. Make sure it's phenomenal.

- Lead with an idea, *not* who you are or what your brand is. In reality, people care about themselves. The reporter wants you to help them write a great story.

- Be creative. Study and use Copyblogger to create a headline that stands out.

Use compelling tools

Use photos, videos, links to source material, and any other in depth resources. Give reporters the help they need to fully report the news you're providing them.

Add links from Youtube or other press clips to help tell your story.
Make it easy for the reporter and your blog or product will land the press.

Use This Press Release Generator

 FREE Press Release Generator to help write a great press release.

Proofread

I did not major in English. I will be totally honest with you right now and say that I am also not the greatest with grammar. If you are, that is wonderful. If you are not, then may I suggest you find someone who is. If you have a friend, or can afford to hire a professional editor, you will be amazed with the mistakes they are able to point out. Trust me I know. My book was revised by

my two editors, Best Foot Forward & Tamara from
www.dgmommy.com . If you are in need of an editor, they are
fabulous.

You may contact Tamara from Aspiring Domestic Goddess
Mommy here : www.dgmommy.com
email: adgmommy@gmail.com

And you may contact Best Foot Forward here:
editsbyBFF@aol.com

How To Find Products To Review

In order to get companies to notice your blog, you need to have these few simple things in place:

A review policy - a short paragraph stating that you receive products to review and are sometimes paid, but the opinions are all your own.

You may want to include what your procedure is. Do you send products back after you review them? Most don't. How you'd like them shipped (unopened), and things of that nature.

A disclosure policy. This is a very cool tool. Just fill in the multiple choice and it generates your own personal disclosure policy-
http://disclosurepolicy.org/generator/generate_policy

Add your contact information. Always make it easy for prospective companies to find you.

I've recruited my awesome girlfriend, Lindsay, from Lindsay Blogs to give you her take on finding products to review. She's very knowledgeable and I know you'll love what she has to say:

If I were to think of a list of the most frequently asked questions that I get from beginning bloggers, right at the top of the list would be, "**How do you get companies to send you products to review?**"

In all honesty, it's not nearly as difficult as you think. Yes, larger companies with more expensive products do want to see some higher visitor numbers and page rankings than most starting bloggers can offer, but that doesn't mean there are *no* companies you can work with. Start small and dream big!

I cannot tell you how many product reviews I have landed just by telling a company with products that I'd love the opportunity to work with them. The worst that can happen is they don't reply or they say, "no."

Who Do I Email?

The first part of asking, however, is knowing *whom to ask*. That's really the biggest problem for most bloggers (new and experienced). Finding the right e-mail address to make sure your pitch gets seen can be a daunting task, but a few searches should get you there. Just do a quick Google for:

- "Company X PR Contact" or you can replace "PR" with "Media"

- "Company X Press Release" – You can often find a PR representative's contact information in the top corner of the press release, or sometimes at the bottom.

- Sign up for the company's media outreach mailing list – Almost every single one of the emails you receive from this type of list will have a contact name and email attached to a particular product.

What Do I Say?

Once you know whom to contact, you need to know what to write. There is really no hard definition of a perfect pitch letter, but there are a few key things to keep in mind when writing one:

- **Keep it simple** – We've all heard the K.I.S.S. rule (Keep It Simple, Stupid). PR reps are busy and if they see a wall of text coming at them, they are more likely to hit "Delete" than to sit there and read through your novel to learn about your blog. Make your initial pitch a one- or two-paragraph e-mail (and by "paragraph" I mean 2-3 sentences), just introducing yourself and offering up your services.

- **Make it less about your <u>request</u> and more about your <u>offer</u>** – Companies are asked for free products all the time. Don't make this a pitch about what they can do for you, but rather what *you* can do for *them*. Do you have a strong following on Facebook? **Tell them!** Do you have a very engaged and active readership? **Tell them!** This email should be all about how you can help the company get their product seen by the masses!

- **Leave the stats out of it** – I know this seems like an odd thing to leave out, but trust me – you won't regret it. Out of the hundreds of pitches I have sent out (without including my stats), I have only been asked to provide them *maybe* 5% of the time. PR reps care less about your stats than you think. Having a great review reach 100 moms who are truly interested in the product is far better than that same review reaching 1,000,000 people who could not possibly care less about the product.

Then What?

First off, be prepared to hear the word "No" a lot. It's not a reflection of your blog or your skills. That's just the way it goes in the world of product reviews. You are going to hear "No" or absolutely nothing back a lot more than you hear "Yes."

But, when you do get those "yes" emails flowing back in, **build those relationships**. Remember, these are not just faceless emails – there is a person on the other end. If you build those relationships with the PR rep on the other end, you are likely to get more reviews from that same rep <u>or</u> be recommended to other reps looking for bloggers.

Lastly, **do what you promised**. If you told the rep you would have their review up and ready to go by February 9th, then you had better have that review up and ready by February 9th. This is how you gain a reputation as a solid professional blogger. If, for some reason, you are unable to make a deadline, just let the rep know. Remember, they are human – they understand life happens. But, they also have a job to do and if you're not helping them by doing your part, you will likely not get a second chance.

That's it?

Yes, that really is it. That is how bloggers get their start in the world of reviews. Eventually, you won't have to send out any pitches – they will all come to you! Even then, keep these tips in mind so that you can continue to grow as a blogger and hit the goals you have set for yourself. No one can stop you, except YOU!

Lindsay Chung is the owner and blogger behind *Lindsay Blogs* – your resource for product reviews, giveaways, and life stories, all with a humorous and fun take. She lives in Metro Atlanta with her husband and two girls.

Final Thoughts

As I stated at the beginning, I've spent hundreds of hours and quite a few months crafting this book for you. None of the information in this book will help just by reading it. You have to DO it. I know you will. I believe in you.

Please don't forget to comment and visit me on Facebook & Twitter.

I'd like to thank my other contributors, Amy Lynn Andrews from Blogging With Amy for allowing us to check out her in depth blog button tutorial and Lindsay from Lindsay blogs for teaching you how to pitch for reviews.

Now, go and make your blog the most amazing blog on the planet and

GET FAMOUS!

Mega Resource Page

My Personal Favorites:

www.fiverr.com Anything you can imagine you can find here for $5 bucks.

www.odesk.com Outsource every type of technical work you can imagine. (be careful posting your website; it can get spammy)

http://www.linkyfollowers.com/ -This was created by my good friend, Brent Riggs, the original master of the Linky Tool. This cool widget takes the place of Google Friend Connect and is packed with features. Be sure to visit.

Beginner Blog Basics: Another excellent resource is Darren Rowse's newly updated *Problogger 31 Days To A Better Blog*.

Just click the link in blue to read this post he wrote a while ago *Problogger 31 days to a better blog*.

Media & Press Release - The Top Two are the Most Important

http://www.helpareporter.com/ Pitch journalists your stories and receive what they are looking for most.

http://www.reporterconnection.com/

http://www.bmyers.com/public/539.cfm A really cool free press release generator -just fill in the blanks and you have your press release! Couldn't be easier-

24-7PressRelease.com – Free release distribution with ad-support

1888PressRelease.com – Free distribution, paid services gives you better placement and permanent archiving.

ClickPress.com – Distributes to sites like Google News and Topix.net. Gold level will also get you to sites like LexisNexis.

EcommWire.com – Focuses on e-commerce. Requires you to include an image, 3 keywords, and links.

Express-Press-Release.com – Free distribution company with offices in 12 states.

Free-Press-Release.com – Easy press release distribution for free; more features for paid accounts.

Free-Press-Release-Center.info – Distributes your release, offers a web page with one keyword link to your site. Pro upgrade will give you three links, permanent archiving, and more.

I-Newswire.com – Allows for free distribution to sites and search engines. Premium membership differs only slightly with added graphics.

NewswireToday.com – All the usual free distribution tools. Premium service includes logo, product picture and more.

PR.com – Not only will they distribute your press releases, but you can also set up a full company profile.

PR9.net – Ad supported press distribution site.

PR-Inside.com – European-based free press release distribution site.

PRBuzz.com – Completely free distribution to search engines, news sites, and blogs.

PRCompass.com – Distribute your press release with a free or paid version, others can vote it up ala Digg style.

PRUrgent.com – Not only distributes your release but attempts to teach you how to write one, and even offers download samples for you to work with.

Press-Base.com – Submit your release for free and get on their front page in the category of your choice.

PressAbout.com – A free press release service formatted as a blog.

PressMethod.com – Free press release distribution no matter what, but extra services based on the size of your contribution.

PRLeap.com – Free distribution to search engines, newswires, and RSS feeds. Fee based bumps get you better placement.

PRLog.org – Free distribution to Google News and other search engines.

TheOpenPress.com – Gives free distribution for plain formatted releases, fees for HTML-coded releases.

Where to Find Products to Review and Get Paid to Blog

http://momspark.net/

http://www.momdot.com/

http://www.tomoson.com/

http://socialspark.com/

http://business2blogger.com/

http://clevergirlscollective.com/

Glam- This is an ad network they are a little more exclusive but you can try and apply with them as well.

Sites That Pay You To Blog:

http://www.hongkiat.com/blog/sites-that-pays-you-to-blog/

Sponsored Reviews

Earn cash by writing honest reviews about our advertisers' products and services. Write reviews in your own tone and style, and gear them to your audience's interest.

Link Post

Unlike some other services, we pay our Partners up to 70% for each LinkPost written. Access to thousands of advertisers hungry for reviews. A variety of payment options. Receive payouts monthly by check, PayPal, direct deposit, or Wire. Automated advertising management. An easy way to sell paid blog posts.

Review Me

Get paid $20 – $200 to review products and services on your site. You control what you review.

Shvoong

The more abstracts you post at Shvoong, the more chances to attract readers. Create links to your abstract elsewhere (on blogs, forums, your personal homepage, or other sites). Spread the word by joining our "Invite a friend" and/or "Affiliates" programs and earn bonuses equivalent to the invited members royalties, up to $100 for every new writer.

PayPerPost

PayPerPost is an incredible new self-service marketplace that allows you to get paid to blog about the products, services and websites you love. You can easily earn $500 per month or more with your current blog!

Be A Guide (About.com)

All About.com Guides are <u>freelancers</u> who work online and set their own schedules, giving them the flexibility to log on from anywhere in the world whenever they have the time. With no timesheets to fill out and no timecards to punch, working for About.com gives you the flexibility to write when you want, even if you have a full-time day <u>job</u>.

BlogBurner

So here's how it works:

- You create an account with us.
- You create an account with Google Adsense.
- You login and write content to your "blog" on our site.
- You try to write as often as you can.
- We publish your content to our site.
- We serve ads on the pages that have your content.
- Half the time you make money on the ads. Half the time we do.

Blogitive

Once you are approved to the Blogitive system, you are given access to opportunities from companies to post about their news releases. You are paid per posting.

Blogsvertise

Once approved, your blog goes into the assignment queue. The blogsvertise administrator then assigns writing tasks for what our advertisers want you to mention in your blog.

BOTW Media

If you are an experienced writer and/or an avid blogger, can write passionately about a topic, and enjoys working as part of a group, you may be a good candidate for a BOTW Media author.

Creative Weblogging

Get paid to blog with us at Creative Weblogging! We are one of the largest blog networks, with over 135 blogs in five languages.

DayTipper

If you have a tip that is insightful, helpful, and original, we will publish it and pay you $3 (US). You write the content. We share it with the world.

Digital Journal

Unlike most websites where bloggers post for free (and the company takes in all the ad revenue), DigitalJournal.com shares a portion of its advertising revenue with all Citizen Journalists. With an always-growing cash pool, every single Citizen Journalist gets a chance to compete for a share of the cash pot. The more you contribute, the more you earn.

Helium

Earn a share of the advertising money earned here at Helium. If you write well, and write often, you earn even more recognition and reward.

LoudLaunch

If your blog and interests are aligned with an advertiser's campaign then you can do your own research and write about them in exchange for pay—not in exchange for a pre-determined outcome but for a fair assessment.

Squidoo

Every lens carries Google AdSense ads. Those are used to generate royalties for the whole co-op (ie, everyone gets a cut). If you want to increase your direct royalties, though, you should consider adding commercial modules that the visitors to your lenses will appreciate.

Wise Bread

WiseBread.com is one of the top 5 <u>personal finance</u> blogs. We give our bloggers 100% of the advertising revenue they earn on their blog posts.

b5media

We'll pay you to write about what you love. We're the one of the largest blog networks in the world. We want to be the biggest. Want to help? It's easy to apply.

30 FREE IMAGES FOR YOUR BLOG:

Visit this website for a list of free images to use on your blog.
http://websearch.about.com/od/bestwebsites/tp/free-images.htm

FREE Blog Backgrounds:

http://leelou-blogs.com/

http://www.thecutestblogontheblock.com/free/free-backgrounds.html

http://shabbyblogs.com/

http://www.bloggerbuster.com/2011/01/free-blogger-backgrounds-and-textures.html

Sites To Find Web Designers And Help

http://www.craigslist.org/about/sites/

I have found website designers for $35 an hour using this site. I post ads myself for my projects as well as scan other services that people offer. My next eBook may be filled with money saving tips for your blog or business. I have learned so much with the design of my blog. I want you to know you should never pay in the thousands for any project if you have a new blog it's just not necessary. I trust these tips will help to save you as much money as they have me or more.

Bonus Feature
SEO Tips That Won't Make Your Eyeballs Fall Out

I say this because when I hear "SEO" I just want to run and bury my head under a pillow. However it's a key part to your success, so I'll just share a few simple tips that won't overwhelm you and that have worked for me.

Please keep in mind I am not an SEO expert. However, there are many of them out there, so keep searching to learn more.

• Write content that's inviting. The idea is to get people to share your content with others and have them link back to it. When you have natural links leading back to your site, it improves your SEO.

• Optimize the page so search engines know what's its about. You can learn more about this by searching Google " How to optimize my page for SEO"

• Use Social media sites like like Stumble Upon, Twitter and Facebook, and Pinterest to get readers to notice your content and link to it, driving more traffic to your blog. Be active on social media.

- Use Google Key Word Search Tool

For more information on how to use this key word search tool, simply Google "How to use key word search tool"

• Guest Post. If you guest post on established blogs, it allows you to raise your profile and add links back to your own site. It's a great method and used by many people.

• When you write a byline for your guest post, make sure you use anchor text with the search term that you want associated with your blog. If you are posting on a popular blog that will help you to get a high Google Page Rank. For example my byline may read:

Lisa Cash Hanson Writes for Mompreneur Mogul, a blog that shares blogging tips, & ways to make money blogging. Lisa loves to share advice that will make your blog soar.

You can see I used the anchor text "blogging tips" in place of my website name and added the following link: www.mompreneurmogul.com.

When people search for blogging tips this technique will improve my ranking.

Content + Promotion =Links
 Links = higher rankings on search engine sites.

Ping Your Blog

Blog Traffic. If you'd like more visitors, make sure to PING YOUR BLOG!

Why do you NEED to ping your blog? Well because even though you have built it – *they WON'T come* until you tell the search engines how to find you. That's what pinging your blog is all about. It makes your blog say "Look at me, look at me, here I am!" and get noticed by search engines.

Here is a cool list of places (free ping submission services) to ping your blog.

FeedShark

Pingler

ping o matic

Auto Pinger

Ping That Blog

Blog buzzer

A Small Window Into My World

As an added bonus, here is the exact pitch that I used to get Yahoo to fly to Las Vegas and do a show based around my tips. The original pitch asked for those who had money saving tips. For Yahoo-

Pitch Title: Our Family is Perfect I Impersonated Shania Twain Now Stay At Home Mom

Pitch Contents: Hi, our family would be perfect for your interview! Plus with my background we are the ultimate Vegas family.

This is our family: Chad, Matilda, (9months old, & myself,) (I've excluded photos)

I had been a very successful Vegas impersonator touring as Shania Twain, Cher Madonna and others but I quit to become a stay at home mom and raise my daughter.

That cut our income yearly by $xx,xxx. (this has been omitted for the purpose of maintaining our privacy) A huge cut.

I didn't know if we would make it. Through a series of tricks I found (calling my cell phone company & getting my bill reduced, switched insurance companies and a few other things) I was able to save our household as much as $250 a month.

Not only am I able to stay home and raise my daughter but I only have one payment left on my Lincoln Navigator. Both of the cars we own will now be paid in full.

 I've also launched Mompreneur Mogul, a successful mom blog where I sell informational products and give blogging tips to other moms.

Recently, I created an awesome baby product which is in the manufacturing phase.

Even though our finances have been cut dramatically we are really soaring high :)

My contact info is below & my number is ###-####

Thanks for your time Feel free to check out my blog, as well. if you Google

"Lisa Cash" you'll see tons of photos of when I impersonated those stars :)

As a result of that pitch, the crew flew from NY to LV and filmed us for the day. We appeared on Yahoo Finance with 1 million potential viewers, and because I asked if my blog could be featured, this was the article underneath the video with a link to my blog.

Living on 50% Less
By Lisa Cash Hanson

Not that long ago, finding crazy-unique ways to save money was never on my list of things to do. I was working as a celebrity impersonator in Las Vegas, and the dough kept rolling in. But suddenly, my husband and I received the greatest news of our lives – we were expecting a baby!

There comes a moment in every successful soon-to-be mom's pregnancy when she asks herself, "Do I keep working this job…or stay home to raise my child?" When I rolled this question around in my head, I knew my singing and traveling gypsy days were numbered. I loved performing, but being able to spend time with my daughter meant so much more.

So, I hung up my rhinestones and feather headdresses, and immediately went into savings mode. We'd now be living on one income, a whopping 50% less than we were used to. Such a dramatic change in our finances would require both some creative thinking -- and some serious negotiations.

Some people like to use the word "budget" -- but I prefer "adjustment." Small, incremental changes that over time, add up to a lot of savings! We've "adjusted" in a bunch of ways: my salon visits and weekly mani-pedis are ancient history of course, and even my husband has found ways to "adjust." He's traded in an expensive hobby (drag racing) for a more affordable past-time (target practice – and instead of buying bullets… he makes his own!).

Here are some of my all-time favorite strategies for managing bills and saving money:

· **Call your service providers and ask if they're running specials:** Over a period of several months I went from a cell phone bill of $175 to $85 using this method – and believe me, my plan has all the perks! The cable company? They said, "Sure, we can give you a $5 monthly credit." Why? Who knows. Probably because I asked.

· **Switch car insurance companies:** Do your research because you don't want inferior coverage -- but this one little tip is currently saving us about $150 a month.

· **Refuse to pay credit card membership fees:** Many times these fees go unnoticed but when I called my credit card company to tell them I didn't want to pay this monthly fee, they offered to remove it.

· **Pay bills on time:** Sometime we let bills slide out of laziness. I've done that. But I've also learned this one little "slip up" can cost a LOT in late fees: $35 here, $20 there. And who'd willingly burn up a 20 dollar bill?

· **Use coupons that make sense for *you*:** I can't hang with those moms on the Extreme Couponing shows -- but when I find a coupon that works for my family, I use and use again! We found a coupon for our grocery store that gets us $20 off a $100 grocery bill -- each time we shop. My husband buys diapers at our local Baby Store instead of the grocery store because they offer a gift certificate with purchase. These are the expenses that add up quickly in our household, and so we go out of our way for the deal.

· **Get creative:** I knew that if I could combine my skills as a writer and businesswoman, I could share what I've learned with other moms! Last year I launched my blog, Mompreneur Mogul – and even started designing my own baby products. Not only are these projects incredibly rewarding for me as I raise my daughter, they're incrementally bringing additional income into the household – which is only going to help secure our future in years to come.

These simple strategies have helped my family adjust to living on *half* of what we did before, allowing me to stay home with Matilda -- and for that, we're grateful.

With Much Gratitude

I would like to thank the following people for their contributions and amazing support:

My Editors: Tamara Vellozzo - Freelance writer/editor, fellow blogger, and my new amazing friend. Tamara I cannot thank you enough for all the time and effort you spent. You are amazing! Thank you Thank you. adgmommy@gmail.com

Grace Kone editsBFF@aol.com

Grace is also an accomplished author. Seventeen of her romance and mystery novels can be found under the name *Blaire Bancroft* on Amazon, Amazon Kindle, Smashwords, Nook, Sony & Palm.

Visit her website www.blairbancroft.com
Blog http://mosaicmoments.blogspot.com/

Facebook & Linkedin Grace Kone   Twitter @blairbancroft

Amy Lynn Andrews from www.bloggingwithamy.com

Lindsay Chung from www.lindsayblogs.com

My sweet friend and x-band mate, Susie. Grace is her mother.

Thank you for contributing to the success of this book. Amy, thank you for allowing us to showcase your blog button tutorial.

Lindsay, thank you for the great article on *How Do You Get Companies To Send You Products*.

Jerry Shoemaker from Shoemoney for his link: *Getting Press For Your Website, Application, or Service*

Darren Rowse for his link: *31 Days To A Better Blog*

I would also like to give a shout out to the awesome women at Vegas Bloggers Community : http://vegasbloggers.net/

Please note that there are many links used in the writing of this eBook. The internet is constantly changing and if for any reason a link is no longer active it may mean the service has been discontinued. Thank you for your understanding.

About The Author

Lisa Cash Hanson is very familiar with the term *Get Famous*. She has spent most of her life touring the world and traveling as a professional Las Vegas Celebrity singer, performing as some of the most famous women in recording history. After the birth of her daughter she hung up her rhinestones and feather headdress and decided to settle into mommy hood.

Never one to slow down for very long, she quickly launched Mompreneur Mogul in anticipation of an amazing new baby product she was creating.

Suddenly, the blog became crazy popular and started to take on a life of its own. Lisa soon found herself mentoring other moms and creating products to enable them to market and create the *Most Amazing Blog On The Planet*. That was the beginning of *Get Famous*.

Lisa still sings professionally, however, she no longer tours. She is a freelance writer, a regular contributor on popular parenting websites, a Mompreneur and a sought-after public speaker. She has made Television appearances on numerous outlets including most recently, Yahoo! Shine, a female-focused website boasting as many as 31 million unique visitors a month.

If you are interested in booking Lisa for your upcoming events, contact her via lisa@mompreneurmogul.com